It Is Hot!

by Susanna Fallon
illustrated by Linda Bronson

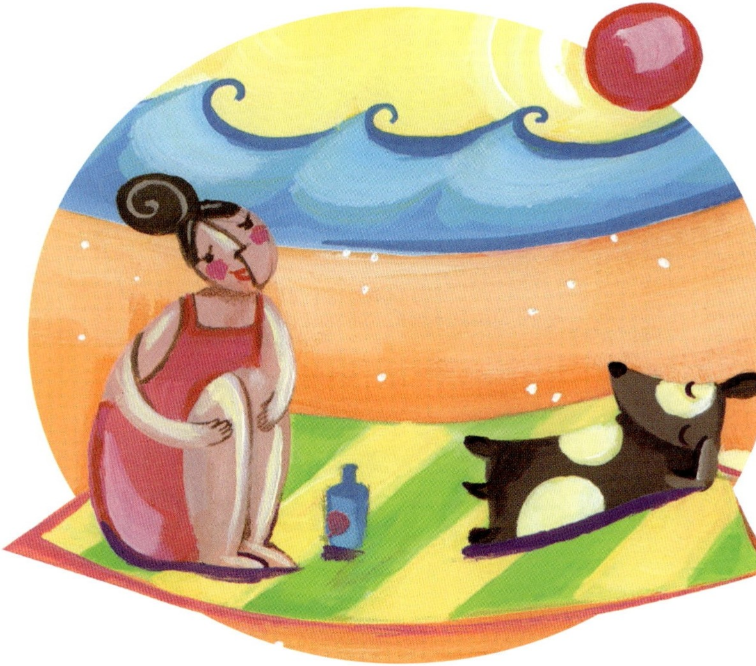

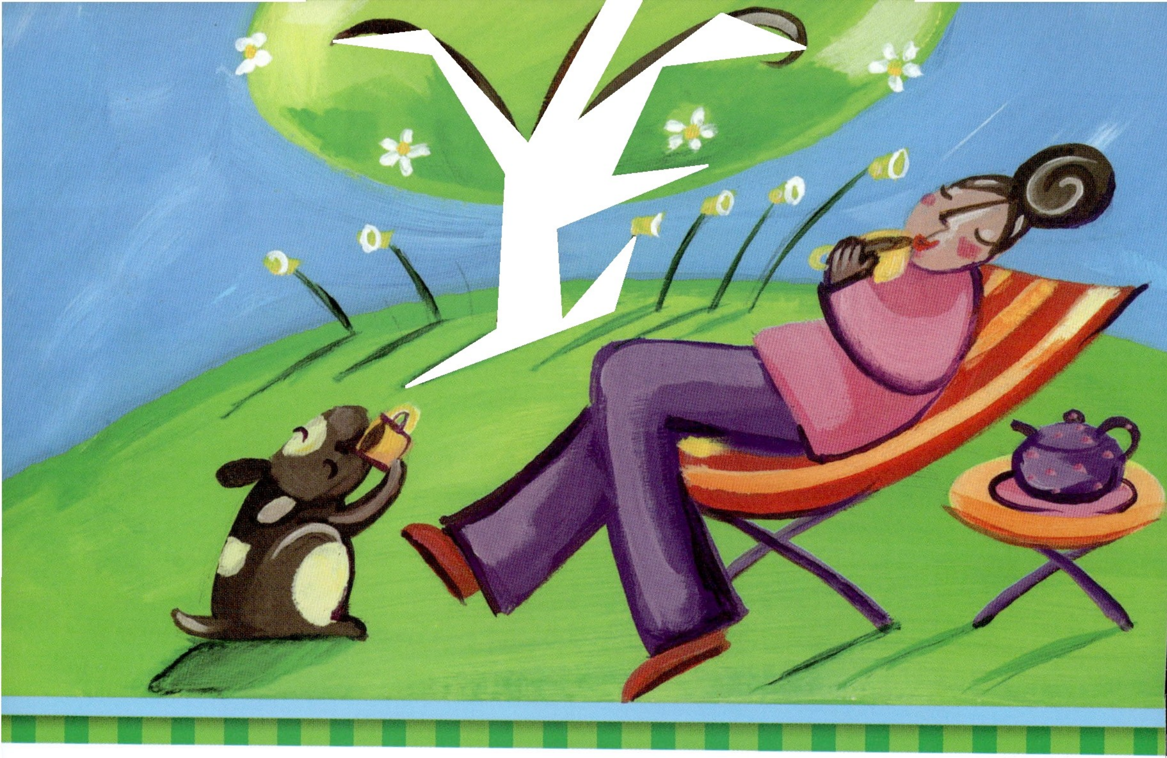

The 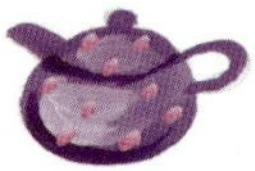 tea is hot.

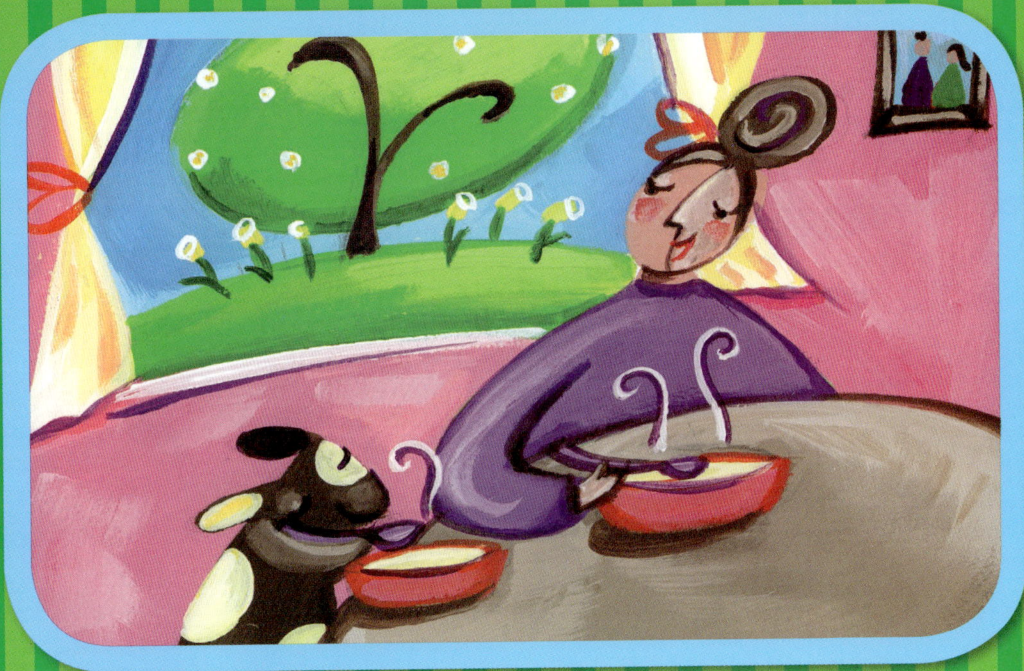

The  soup is hot.

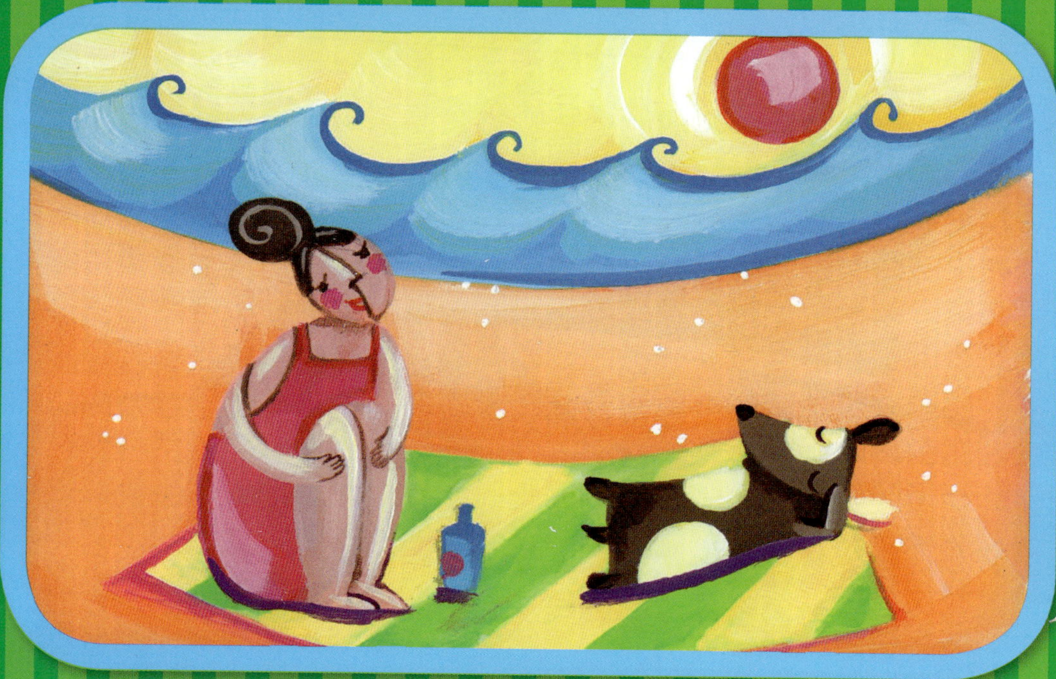

The 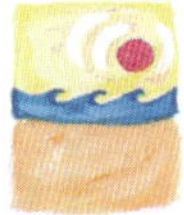 beach is hot.

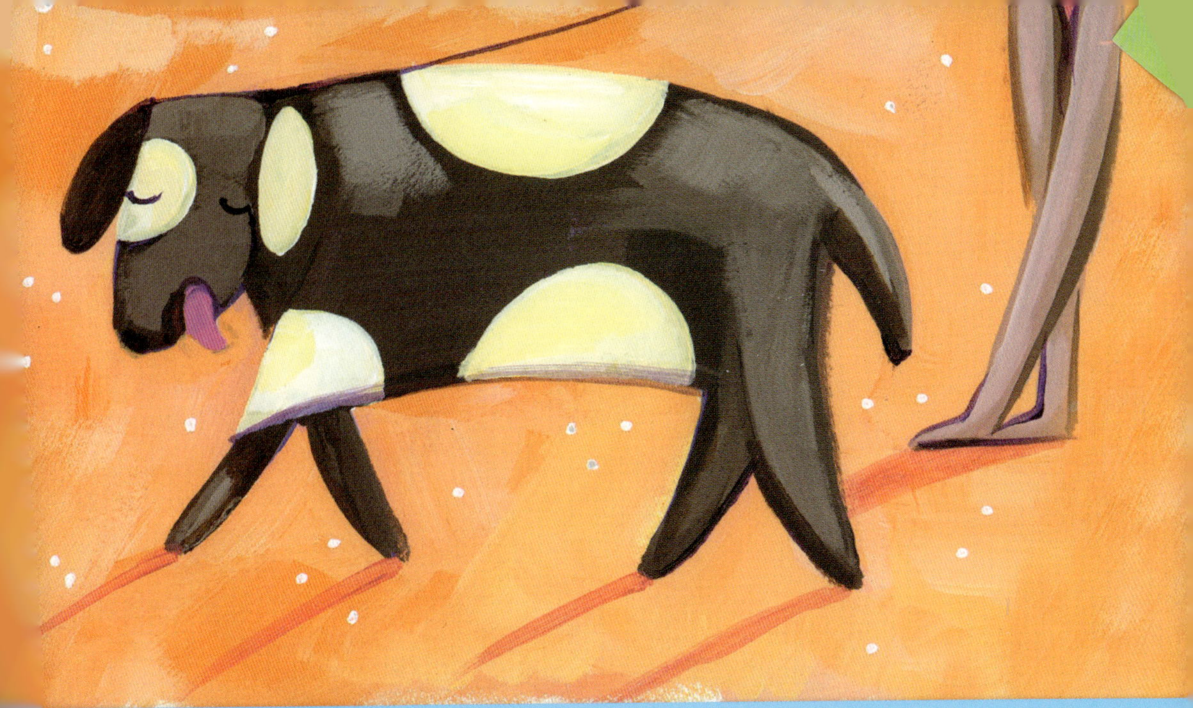

The 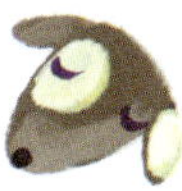 dog is hot.

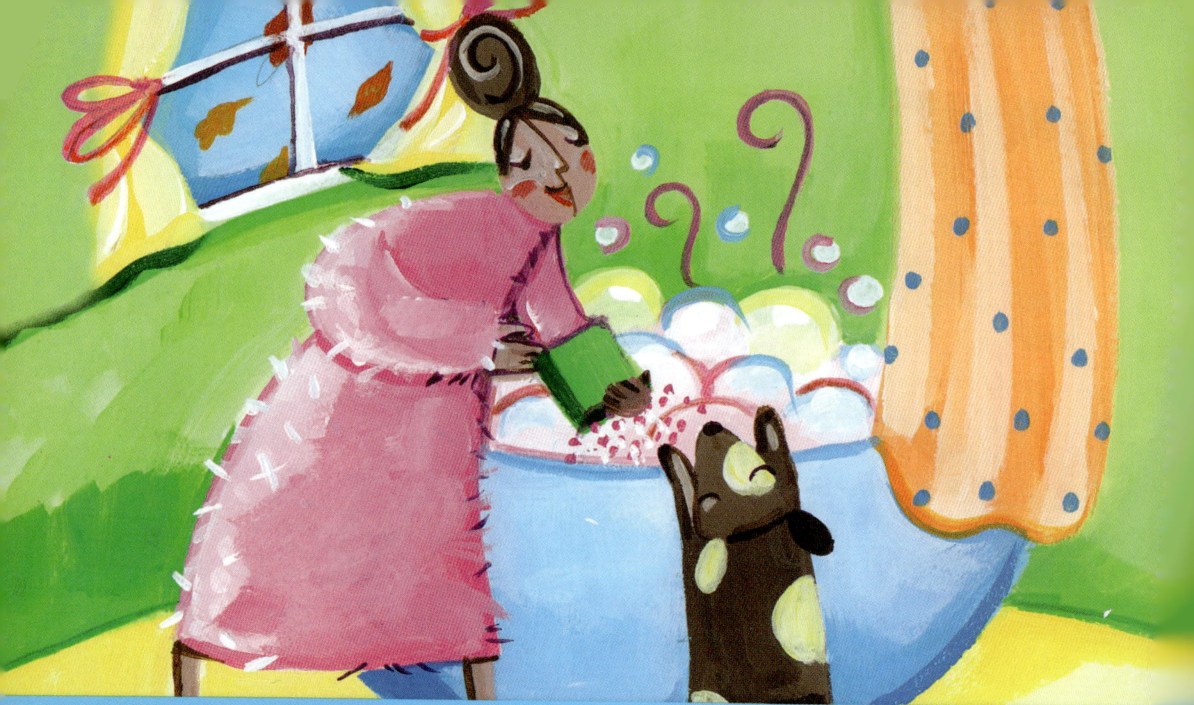

The  tub is hot.

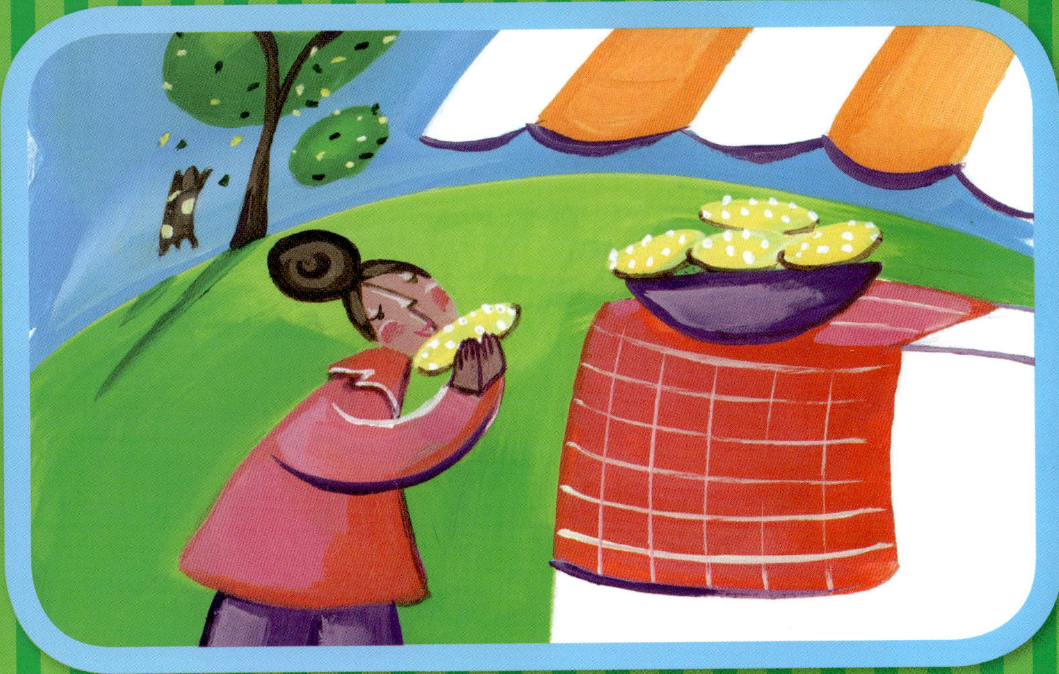

The  corn is hot.

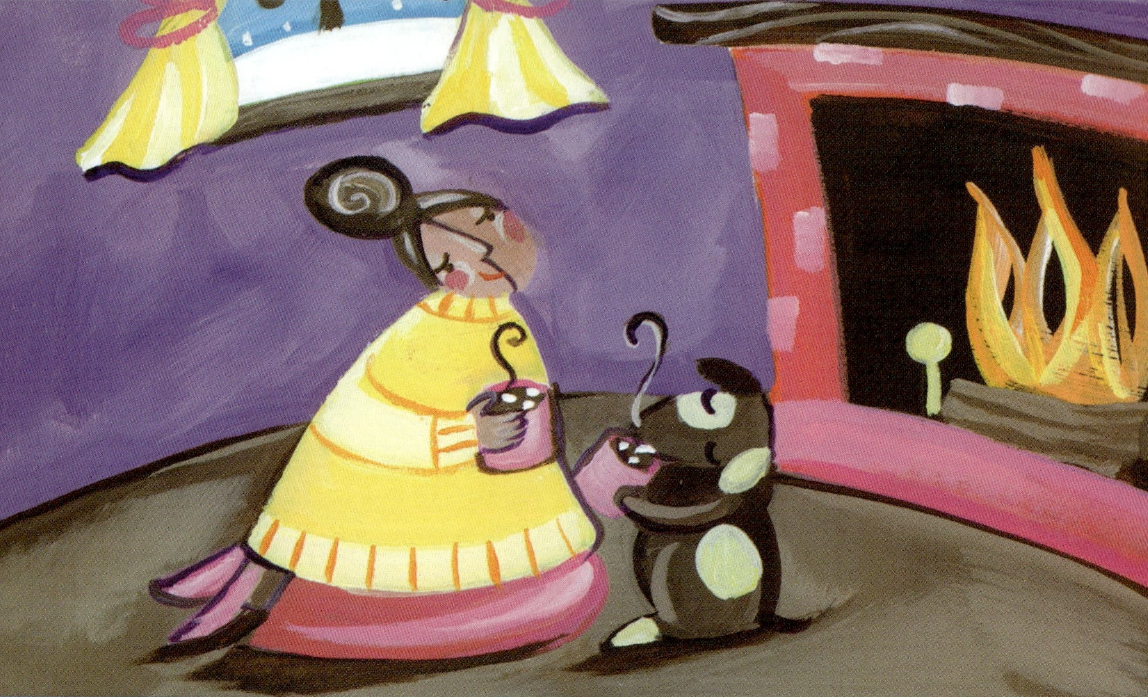

The  mug is hot, hot, hot.